*For naturalists young, old, or anything in between.*



ISBN: 979-8-218-48502-3

Published by Anomura Book Company.

# Introduction

Thanks to billions of years of evolution—the process that has resulted in all life—planet Earth is extremely biodiverse (bye-oh-die-VURSS). That means our planet is home to a great variety of different organisms and species, also known as living things. This book features a handful of those living things, specifically animals. There are many well-known animals that have held the spotlight for a while, like the graceful Giraffe or the majestic Bald eagle, but there are so many lesser-known animals that are just as remarkable and breathtaking. The animals in this book are just a few examples of incredible lifeforms that have long inhabited our planet but that might be new to many readers.

# For the Reader

For new nature lovers: this book may introduce you to some new concepts or ideas, and there will likely be some words which you have never read before. You will learn what these terms mean by reading about the amazing animals in this book.

For experienced nature lovers: even if you may have heard of a few of these animals before, you will likely still learn something new about each of them and biology in general. Or, you might just enjoy the artwork.

For everyone: this book is meant not only to educate, but to inspire a sense of wonder for the natural world and curiosity to learn more about it.

# ARCHERFISH

## *The truest aim in freshwater.*

Found in fresh bodies of water from Southeast Asia to Australia, the ordinary-looking Archerfish is actually an incredible hunter. Interestingly, the Archerfish hunts for land-dwelling prey, specifically insects. If the Archerfish spots an insect overhead, it will shoot a jet of water from out of its mouth to knock the unlucky bug into the water where the Archerfish can eat it. It does this with incredible accuracy, often not needing more than one well-aimed shot to hit its target.

## Did you know?

The Archerfish isn't born knowing how to shoot water from its mouth. It learns how to from watching other Archerfish.

The Archerfish hitting an insect with a jet of water.

# NAKED MOLE-RAT

## *Teamwork makes the dream work.*

The life of the Naked mole-rat is just as interesting as its appearance. Even though it is a mammal, the Naked mole-rat acts more like an ant or a bee. It lives in East Africa in underground colonies with one queen mole-rat who is the only female who gives birth. The rest of the colony members are workers who dig tunnels, look for food, defend against predators, and take care of the queen's young. This system is known as eusociality (yu-soh-shee-AL-it-ee) and mole-rats, like the Naked mole-rat, are the only species of eusocial (yu-SOH-shull) mammals.

## Did you know?

The Naked mole-rat is able to live for almost 40 years, making it the longest living species of rodent.

The underground tunnels of a Naked mole-rat colony.

# EMERALD GREEN SEA SLUG

## *You are what you eat.*

Not only does the Emerald green sea slug look like a cross between a sea slug and a leaf, it acts like one, too. While it is one hundred percent animal, the Emerald green sea slug has the incredible ability to make its own food using sunlight through a process called photosynthesis (foh-toh-SIN-thuh-siss), something usually only plants can do. The algae it eats is full of chloroplasts (KLOR-oh-plasts), tiny microscopic (my-croh-SCOP-ick) structures that help turn light into sugars. When the slug consumes the algae, it absorbs the chloroplasts into its own body and photosynthesises on its own. This ability is known as kleptoplasty (KLEP-toh-plass-tee).

## Did you know?

Scientists are still not exactly sure how the Emerald green sea slug is able to maintain its chloroplasts for so long.

The chloroplasts (second from right) in algae (left) and in the Emerald green sea slug (right).

# SANDGROUSE

## A *flying sponge.*

In the dry deserts of Africa, many animals must visit watering holes to get water, and the Sandgrouse is no exception. However, it may encounter a predator that's looking for a snack alongside its drink at the watering hole. That's why the Sandgrouse nests far away from watering holes. While the adult Sandgrouse can simply fly to and from a watering hole and its nest, its flightless chicks cannot. In order to get water to its chicks, the adult Sandgrouse has special belly feathers that can soak up and hold water for the potentially miles long flight back to its nest. When the parent returns, the chicks will drink the water from their parent's soaked belly feathers.

### Did you know?

Due to the lack of trees in its environment, the Sandgrouse nests on the ground. This type of nest is called a scrape.

The scrape or nest of the Sandgrouse.

# DIVING BELL SPIDER

## An eight-legged SCUBA diver.

As its name suggests, the Diving bell spider is able to dive underwater. While most spiders live only on land, the Diving bell spider will actually spend most of its life in bodies of freshwater in Europe and parts of Asia thanks to some incredible abilities. This spider spins an underwater air bubble out of silk, attaches it to an aquatic plant, and lives in it. When it gets hungry, it leaves its bubble to dive for prey. It is able to do this because as it exits the bubble, a smaller air bubble stays on the spider's abdomen (AB-duh-min) which acts like an oxygen tank underwater.

## Did you know?

Hairs on the Diving bell spider's body repel water, keeping the air bubble around it.

The Diving bell spider leaving its bubble for prey.

# AYE-AYE

## *Knock knock, anyone home?*

Perhaps the only thing freakier than the eyes of the Aye-aye (EYE-eye) are its hands. Found in the forests of Madagascar, the Aye-aye has strangely bony fingers, the boniest of them being its middle finger. This finger is extremely helpful to the Aye-aye when hunting for its prey: grubs. Specifically, the Aye-aye uses its middle finger to tap rapidly (up to eight times per second) on the wood in its forest home to try and find hollow spaces where grubs have tunneled. Once it finds such a spot, it chews open the wood and uses its middle finger again to scoop out its late-night snack.

## Did you know?

This tapping is a form of echolocation (EK-oh lo-KAY-shun) which the Aye-aye uses to find prey, much like how the bat uses echolocation to find its way around in the dark.

The Aye-aye tapping a tree with its boney middle finger to find where a grub is hidden.

# BOMBARDIER BEETLE

*Beetle on the outside, mad scientist on the inside.*

Found in woodlands throughout the world, this harmless-looking beetle uses a potent and powerful defense mechanism. When threatened, the Bombardier (bawm-ber-DEER) beetle creates an explosive chemical reaction in its abdomen (AB-duh-min). Three different chemicals come together to form an exothermic (eck-soh-THUR-mick) reaction which means it produces heat and pressure. The pressure forces the mixture out of an opening in the tip of the Bombardier beetle's abdomen. This results in a near boiling toxic spray being released in quick spurts right at the threat.

## Did you know?

The opening on the Bombardier beetle's abdomen can swivel to get a better shot at its attacker.

*The part of the Bombardier beetle's body that starts the chemical reaction to create the hot spray.*

# POTOO
## *Bird, frog, or tree branch?*

Something about the face of the Potoo (poh-TOO) is almost alien. Its huge eyes can appear almost entirely black or yellow, and when its wide beak is open, it looks a little like a frog. Despite its eye-catching features, this bird can make itself practically invisible when hiding from predators. All it needs to do is sit still with its eyes and mouth closed and its head pointed up. By doing this, the Potoo perfectly camouflages itself with the tree branch it's perched on, tricking its predators by hiding in plain sight.

### Did you know?

Unlike most birds, the Potoo does not make a nest. Instead, it lays its egg in a hole in a tree branch or on top of a tree stump.

The Potoo blending
in to its environment.

# COCONUT CRAB

*A great thing with a small beginning.*

The largest land-dwelling arthropod (AR-throh-pod)—the group of animals containing insects, crabs, lobsters, and shrimp—is actually a giant species of hermit crab called the Coconut crab that lives on tropical islands from East Africa to Australia. It can grow to an incredible three feet wide and weigh up to nine pounds. Surprisingly, it starts off life as plankton, less than a quarter of an inch long. Over time, it grows and finds empty snail shells to live in as it makes its way to the shore. Eventually, the Coconut crab will begin to live only on land and its abdomen will harden until it no longer needs a snail shell for protection.

## Did you know?

The Coconut crab has been observed dropping a coconut from a tree to crack it open to eat the flesh inside.

The growth of the Coconut crab, from plankton (left) to adult (right).

# MIMIC OCTOPUS

## *An aquatic impressionist.*

The seabed of the Indo-Pacific Ocean is mostly sand, which makes it tough for animals to hide from their predators. Luckily, the Mimic octopus figured out a way to trick its predators. Using its eight arms, the Mimic octopus can make itself look like a variety of other, more dangerous sea creatures, a behavior called dynamic mimicry. For example, the Mimic octopus can stick all of its arms out to look like the poisonous Lionfish. Or, by burying itself in the sand while sticking out two of its arms, the Mimic octopus can look like the venomous Sea snake.

## Did you know?

The Mimic octopus also has been observed pretending to be a flatfish, a jellyfish, a crab, and many more animals.

The Mimic octopus mimicking (from left to right) a flatfish, a lionfish, a sea snake, and a jellyfish.

# Conclusion

This book is just a tiny sample of the incredible biodiversity of Earth. There are so many more lesser-known species on Earth that are just as bizarre and awesome as the Bombardier beetle, the Aye-aye, the Potoo, or any other animal in this book. In fact, scientists discover new species everyday. Even if you aren't a scientist yet, as long as you are passionate and curious about the world around us, you too can discover something every single day.

Hi! I'm Jesse Lew. I wrote all the words and drew all the images in this book. I've lived in Southern California most of my life and have loved animals and art for as long as I can remember. Thank you so much for buying a copy of my book!

# Le lama

Jeanne Sélène